Anson County

ALSO BY JOSEPH BATHANTI

POETRY
Communion Partners
The Feast of All Saints
This Metal
Land of Amnesia
Restoring Sacred Art
Sonnets of the Cross

FICTION
East Liberty
Coventry
The High Heart

NONFICTION
They Changed the State: The Legacy of North Carolina's Visiting Artists, 1971-1995

ANSON COUNTY

Poems

JOSEPH BATHANTI

Press 53
Winston-Salem

Press 53, LLC
PO Box 30314
Winston-Salem, NC 27130

First Edition

Copyright © 2013 by Joseph Bathanti

Anson County was originally published in 1989 by William & Simpson,
and again in 2005 by Parkway Publishers.

All rights reserved, including the right of reproduction in
whole or in part in any form except in the case of brief quotations embodied
in critical articles or reviews. For permission, contact author at
editor@Press53.com, or at the address above.

Cover design by Kevin Morgan Watson

Cover art, "A Place Where No One Goes," Copyright © 2013
by Agnieszka Piechocinska, used by permission of the artist.

Author photo by Jan Hensley

Printed on acid-free paper
ISBN 978-1-935708-81-0

For Anson County, especially Joan, Jacob and Beckett

Acknowledgments

The author and the publisher gratefully acknowledge the following publications and their editors in which poems for this volume originally appeared, in some cases earlier versions:

"A Topography of Snakes" in *Appalachian Heritage*; "Easter" in *The Cape Rock*; "Anson County" in *Connecticut Review*; "The Bull" in *The Hollins Critic*; "Advent" in *Kentucky Poetry Review*; "On the Road to White Store" in *The Laurel Review*; "Icons" in *Mississippi Valley Review*; "Icons" in *North Carolina Poetry Society Award Winning Poems*; "Burn Season" and "The George Washington Little House" in *St. Andrews Review*; "Marriage" in *Sojourners*; "Relic" in *Southern Poetry Review*; "Entering an Abandoned House" and "The Sabbath" in *The Texas Review*; "Burn Season" and "The Woods Behind the Tenant Shack" in *Town Creek Poetry*; "The Woods Behind the Tenant Shack" in *Wayah Review*.

Thanks also to the anthologies and their editors in which the following poems appeared:

"Advent" in *Christmas Stories by North Carolina Writers and Twelve Poems, Too*; "Burn Season" and "Easter" in *Earth and Soul: An Anthology of North Carolina Poetry*; "Burn Season" in *Here's to the Land: A Celebration of Sixty Years by the North Carolina Poetry Society*; "The Feast of Stephen" in *The Lives We Seek: Contemporary Poems Inspired by the Saints*; "Sneedsborough" in *Word and Witness: 100 Years of North Carolina Poetry*.

"Signs" first appeared in *The Other Side*.

"Marriage" was awarded First Prize in Poetry by the Associated Church Press, 1988.

Anson County

Introduction: Rediscovering *Anson County*	xiii
Foreword: Signs	xvii
Anson County	3
Advent	5
Icons	7
The Feast of Stephen	8
Here	9
Epiphany	11
The Ghosts of Deer	13
The Woods Behind the Tenant Shack	14
The Fox	16
Sneedsborough	17
Drought	18
The Deer Stand	19
Relic	20
The Bull	21
Burn Season	22
Possums	23
Entering an Abandoned House	24
Sundown at the Ballast Pits	26
The Sabbath	27
The George Washington Little House	29
Disaster Pay	31
Marriage	32
Copperhead	34
A Topography of Snakes	35
Easter	36
On the Road to White Store	37
Cows	38
The Ingram Plantation	39
The Contemplatives of Grassy Island	40
Leaving Anson County	42

Rediscovering *Anson County*
by Heather Ross Miller

We grow up in the middle of places, barely noticing them. Then Joseph Bathanti comes along and tells us such marvelous stories, such truly exciting stories about them, we feel blessed. He didn't grow up here, but he sees the places with clear new dimensions. And leads us into these dimensions with excitement.

For these are poems of excitement in the best sense, that wonderful sense of looking forward, a sense of adventure. He explores Anson County this way, every poem a new discovery or a reaffirmation of our shared discovery. And as we read, following behind him in these adventures and discoveries, he makes companions of us all. We look up and say, "I know that place. That's just how it *is*. That's just what it *does*."

The places tumble through the poems: Walltown, Gum Springs, Whortleberry Creek, Willoughby Trestle, White Store, and Mount Zion. There is no thought to ever doubt their existence. The poet makes them exist in strong detail, their sights and their smells:

> *The house smells of loam and smoke.*
> *Side meat spits in the skillet.*
> *There are corn flowers in a jar*
> *in front of the Byzantine Jesus,*
> *the big red heart pitted with thorns.*

And then the strong personalities that inhabit these places take over our imaginations. These are real people: the wife sleeping in the old house, the baby born, longed-for and adored, the friends who come to hunt and share the land, and the natives, black and white, who share the history of the same land: "... They tell fire / stories and live like saints / off them. They swear / no one was hurt."

People who haunt the house Bathanti lives in, the house within which his son is conceived and later cradled, are as real as the others and share the same history. He writes by candlelight, feeling them move, hearing their testimony, knowing for certain that in this house, in this Anson County, "letters were posted and men loved women; / wayfarers ... dreamt of the future. / Genesis was read Ash Wednesdays / with wild promise ..."

Wild promise, love, and wayfaring. These are strong flavors to find in poems, so bittersweet, so genuine and satisfying. These are the words "to what they alone can hear / in the strange love borne / on the earthback turning."

It is for critics to mock what they call the power of Podunk, the romance of jerkwater, and then to dismiss the poems that make themselves up out of killing copperheads, splitting wood, or climbing old deer stands. But nobody can dismiss these. Bathanti makes it easy to succumb, not to Podunk, not to jerkwater romance, but to an amazingly hard-lived and well-earned experience:

> *This is where the hunter kneels,*
> *camouflaged, introverted;*
> *alone in a way he cannot be elsewhere,*
> *never mistaking anything*
> *for what it is not.*

By the end of the poems, the end of his sojourn in Anson County, a once-vast place that gave birth to many other counties eventually crossing the Smokies and reaching to the Mississippi, Bathanti bids goodbye. He has asked this place for signs, for guides, for directions, and received them all in generous number. He leaves with wife and son, leaves Anson County, "our middle ground" and they "spin for the last time / over roads splayed with tektite / and thistle abloom ..."

And he leaves us, his companion readers, with his quiet but powerful and energetic gifts that have been "the exultation of the ordinary, / the inclusion of our lives in an instant / of light and elevation / whiter than angels."

We are fortunate to have these testimonies of Pennzoil cans and wild viburnum, where blue herons rise out of mistletoe, and a split hickory smells like frankincense. We are lucky such places, such people, exist.

Signs

*"The world will make itself heard in
the most unexpected places."*
—*Thomas Merton,* Opening the Bible

On November 24, 1986, I prayed for a sign. In a faithless age, I longed for no less than something like *the fire out of the midst of a bush* in which Moses had glimpsed his angel. At the time I was living with my wife, Joan, in a haunted house, a charmed house, really, in a place called Grassy Island at the northeast reach of Anson County, North Carolina.

What I know of our former home, the George Washington Little House, is now so mired in romance and the anecdotal that an objective rendering is near impossible. It was one of those houses that engendered wild speculation. Its age varied, depending upon the origin of the account, but it was roughly a hundred years old, built in the classic farmhouse style: two giant rooms stacked on another two, a shotgun hall, steep staircase, big country windows and barn-red shakes. At some point a saltbox had been added, equipping it with kitchen and bathroom. Wide tongue-in-groove pine planks lined the walls and ceilings. Floors of slabbed oak. No conventional heat system, but rather three gargoyle-like woodstoves, only one of which did any real good.

The house's progenitor, George Washington Little, a white, peg-legged planter of some renown, had kept the house as an adjunct to his elegant larger home, fifty yards off, sitting on a promontory overlooking a pond and pasture. This smaller house, it had been suggested, was a private asylum from his wife. George, a Southern

Baptist, was fond of cards, cigars and drinking hard liquor. Conversely, his Southern-born Roman Catholic wife, Ann Horne Little, was decidedly not. Thus the house, in its heyday, was kept as a thoroughly secular retreat. Indeed, while we lived there, it was still known to some in Anson County as George Washington Little's Clubhouse.

The matrimonial dynamic of George and Ann intrigues me. Without resorting to gossip, it seems safe to say that theirs was a highly stylized relationship. Ann guarded the gates of virtue, while George was the avatar of the flesh. The eternal conflict between the sacred and the secular.

On one hand, there were the hasp locks, still on George's upstairs doors, presumably to bar whomever from entering the rooms when he departed them. There were the charred divots his cigars had left in the room where he and his cronies gathered to play poker and drink. A room which set off every parapsychologically sensitive person who entered it.

On the other hand, there stretched endless exquisite gardens sculpted into the landscape by Ann, a former president of the North Carolina Garden Association. Yet the dozen or more genera of cultivated thorns stood as forbidding counterpoints to the sensual wealth of ferns and flowers.

Their marriage, from the standpoint of their respective denominations, strikes me as an inversion of the traditional order. Instead of the Baptist, in this case, George, laying the spiritual foundation, he was the hellion, the public sinner. Meanwhile, the Catholic, Papist, infidel and minority (especially in the deep South of the first half of the twentieth century), embodied all of the zeal and rigor of the fundamentalist Christian.

My interest in this area, that I even noticed it, lies in no small part in the fact that I was raised Catholic and my wife Southern Baptist. Add to that the *coincidence* that we ended up abiding on the very land upon which George and Ann had struck their rather outlandish bargain. Joan and I, in our constant exploration of the acreage, imagined them and even fancied we'd glimpsed them a time or two waltzing along in the blessed space that even lost love keeps sacred. They now reside in the same above-ground tomb at Eastview Cemetery in Wadesboro, and it seems only just to accord them the respect and admiration which that eternal arrangement signals.

Signs

They never had children. When Ann, who survived George by seven years, died, the main house's amazing stores were liquidated on the auction block. The property went to the bank until it finally sold to a young attorney, Fred Poisson, who moved there with his family. The George Washington Little House, sealed front and back with skeleton keys, receded into the forest.

The first time I saw the house I knew I was meant to live there. Two days later, Joan for the first time wandered its huge rooms alone while I stayed outside talking to Fred, our future landlord and great friend, and Big Davis Dunlap, a middle-aged black man who sometimes worked the property. They had just killed a copperhead fifteen feet from the front door. When Joan reappeared, looking enchanted, what I had already known was confirmed. We were going to live in this wild and inexplicable, beautiful barn of a house.

Shortly after moving to Anson County, I made the acquaintance of Charlie Dunlap, the father of Big Davis, mere weeks before he died. Charlie lived with his wife, Lily, and Davis in a tiny dilapidated house down a rutted dirt road a few miles away from us. At some point, during the Depression, I gathered, he had been a companion of George Washington Little. Charlie was a spooked old man, just old, really, somewhere in his nineties, and beat up from living a life close to the bone. He barely spoke, yet he carefully explained that I should fetch a horseshoe and fasten it above our front door. That would keep George, *the peglegged ghost*, said Charlie, without smiling, from entering the house.

We never tacked up a horseshoe, and we never had trouble with spirits, though it more than bears mentioning that Fetzer Mills, our friend who occupied the house after we moved, recounted that he regularly heard shotgun blasts coming from different parts of the house. We did have our spirits, however benign: a sudden flicker not there when turned to; whispers, busy muffled conversations emanating from other rooms, the sudden suspiration of the plank walls.

One night while standing at the brick pillars which led into the property, Joan and I witnessed a fabulous array of blue and red lights spinning like whirligigs, traveling a zig-zag course no aircraft could possibly plot. We watched it for several minutes as it hovered and darted until it burned a phosphorescent hole in the sky and disappeared.

Joseph Bathanti

Everywhere I turned, I saw magic. A half mile east of our house, across a field alternately planted in tobacco, soybeans and wheat, squatted a little box-like, single-spired Baptist church called Mount Zion. No matter the season, it dominated the landscape. Its solitary whiteness, its fixity in the earth and in my mind, suggested at least the notion of a God. We were able to see it perfectly from our upstairs bedroom window. Indeed whenever I was in its proximity, I seemed to be seeing it, if only peripherally. The full moon, in its cycle, would rise and stake itself for hours to the modest steeple. And the church became incandescent with moonlight, throwing a dusky gleam across the crops to the bed where my wife and I slept.

I suppose, without knowing it, I was being evangelized. On the morning of November 24, I set out in a dense fog for my morning run, mizzly rain slicing the drear. I could see only my feet hitting the white line at the remote road's shoulder. Running along, with nothing but faith to assure me that anything else in the world existed, I decided to ask for a sign.

As I ran, I held my hands, palms up, straight out from my shoulders and prayed. I wanted something to happen. I ran for perhaps a hundred yards this way. As I passed Mount Zion Church, a doe rose up at my feet and quickly disappeared in the fog. To me this was altogether remarkable and, although I am a student of happenstance, my psyche is more firmly rooted in the symbolic. Seizing upon the deer as my sign, I rejoiced. Everything was all going to be alright.

Later that night I became aware that the deer was only a precursor to the sign. In a parking lot in Wytheville, Virginia – Joan and I were on our way to spend Thanksgiving with my family in Pittsburgh - my wife informed me that after nine years of marriage we were going to have a baby. A fact, no, a miracle, which forced me into five bottles of beer before I was able to stop jumping up and down.

My wife's pregnancy is really her story. The things that happened to me during it are mere footnotes to the opus, yet extraordinary nonetheless. First of all, our habits changed drastically. Our life acquired a sudden regularity which nothing short of pregnancy could have brought about. We took refuge in our great old house, shielding ourselves against what no longer interested us beyond the door.

Of evenings, Joan, especially in the later months, took to bed quite early. Left to myself, with hours before sleep, I wrote at night by candlelight in our dining room, the old poker parlor. For two or three hours, occasionally more, I'd work in a heat until urged from the room by a faint rustle behind me, what seemed like eyes at the window, or the congregation of ghosts I imagined marching across the winter wheat at my elbow.

Perhaps by sitting in that charged room, in a ring of candles, writing about the house, its former occupants, and the countryside it had been hidden in for years and years, I had all along been invoking ghosts. What I was certain of was that I found a book of poems, later published as *Anson County,* shaping under my hand. A book informed muse-like by the spirit of the dwelling, my sleeping pregnant wife, and the mystery of our unborn child.

A few days after we brought the baby home, Big Davis showed up at our door. I had never really looked into his face until that day, when he stood prayerfully before me, studying the sleeping baby I held. Sweating, whipped by the summer heat, his face mapped with a thousand wisdoms and degradations, he looked older and smaller than the last time I had seen him. He said he'd been *sent by the Lord* to see the child. He stared at the baby with unbridled wonder, then reached for a handkerchief and dabbed at his big eyes. Putting both hands over his heart, he whispered: *Like Jesus in the manger.* Tears ran through the sparse hairs of his face. He couldn't take his eyes from the baby. I couldn't take my eyes from him, noticing for the first time that imbedded in one of his front teeth was a gold star.

On the eve of the day that we left the George Washington Little House and Anson County, my wife and child and I stood in the horse pasture and watched a meteor shower that turned a black sky white as milk for two instants and left the air around us sizzling. Our son, Jacob, was a year old.

Anson County

Anson County

for Joan

You come off the bed
as if expecting me,

take my hand, the morning
of your thirtieth birthday.

Not quite light, perfect
for the movie we've talked of making.

We bicycle the 8 ½ mile loop—
the dogs, one of them blind, lope

ecstatically—gravel
the first two miles,

the ruined church on Savannah Creek,
in a cottonwood swamp that floods

every spring; then a long tar road:
abandoned farmsteads. The last crop—

corn, give-out haggard, by late July,
left to hang into Advent—down

by the Pee Dee, the Ingram Plantation
where Andrew Jackson stopped

to have his hair cut by a slave girl.
The light is like *Petrified Forest*.

You're Bette Davis. I'm Leslie Howard.
You read Francois Villon

and work in a diner in the middle of the desert.
I arrange my own murder

at the hands of Bogart, so you, Davis,
can cash in on my insurance policy.

Tragic beauty.
We avoid making a sad film,

Instead ride into the rising sun
among the regal bucks,

their unfathomable
algorithmic racks, gathered

in homage to you, roaming
McAllister land—

what I had wakened
you so early to witness.

Advent

Shock of wing on water.
Three ring-necks break and spin
into graying and oleander south
and west of us. The blind dog,
haunch high in star thistle
and what's left of the pearl millet,
has come with me to knock down
the Christmas tree. Advent
last he took up with us
and still he lies awake
when other dogs sleep, his eyes
burning like green meteors.

As we navigate the steep pond bank,
he stumbles in horse prints
where they've sunk to the fetlock.
His gait is querulous. Like Isaac,
he intuits the blade is for him.
"Trust," I whisper as I hold
the hatchet over the pink-hearted
cedar and strike.

The heron, having tarried an extra
season in his hideout, lifts up
like an ungainly bomber, flailing
wings and wading legs before jetting
above the mistletoe, surrendering
to us our ceremony of belief.
Over the river when the tree falls,
he is the bluest thing in Anson today.

The dog lies next to the tree
and noses the perfumed marrow.
Smoke chuffs out of the red house
where the woman sleeps,
one hundred years since a child
was born to Grassy Island.
A hawk bellies over fallow fields.
Pilgrims enter Bethlehem
Beneath my knee,
such country exists.

Icons

for Charlie and Lily Dunlap

The door opens slowly.
The house smells of loam and smoke.
Side meat spits in the skillet.
Corn flowers in a jar
in front of the Byzantine Jesus,
the big red heart pitted with thorns.
Framed behind Him: a boy marine,
decorated in dress blues.
Lily peers over bifocals,
one eye on the clouds behind me;
the other, wistful, moiling over
the shrunken future of mercy.
Her hands reach through me,
rope me to her breast.
Lips work at breath and taste
my white cheek. Charlie
appears like a haunt, an arm
loaded with oak, his fedora
mitered to his head. He plants
my fingers in his big brown hand
and pulls me from the doorjamb;
looks beyond me. Surprised,
the pyres of ninety years
shucking his eyes.
The house moves beneath an innocent sky.
Lily smiles and passes
her spatula over us.

The Feast of Stephen

for Mary Charlotte Griffin

A deer stand knifes out of a blackened elm
in a field once held in cotton.
It is the day after Christmas,
the Feast of Stephen,
first martyr, who died praying
for those who stoned him.

On Grassy Island Road,
men with dead quail in their pockets,
lean on pickups, smoke,
and wave grudgingly at passing sedans.

The Star of David spins through a bird sky
that presses the blond earth
with a vast blue sleep,
shadowing tithed tracts
purchased with 18th century sterling
along the Pee Dee and Buffalo Creek.

Corn cribs and cypress cabins
bone into millstone grit;
crumbling grey rock cob;
burlap and buckram;
broken iron, hand-forged
by Ansonville selectmen now buried
in Bethlehem Cemetery.

In All Souls Churchyard,
along its walls of Smith
and Nelme family sandstone,
the stained glass blazes.
Candles burn across the cropland.

Here

An iron bedstead roots
ravaged long-toothed

in the char-eaten carcass.
Redbud and bittersweet push

up through its rusted slumber.
The stairs still stand,

brickwork keen and calcified
where unblackened—

like minimalist sculpture
suggesting flight or welcome.

The door is carbon;
the walls, fossilizing.

Each nail's been squeezed
by fire from its moorings.

Knives and forks eat dirt.
The shutters have blown away.

Twin boys were born
here and still haunt

the back roads
where no one minds them.

Their lives are accidents.
They slept right through it.

One says lightning, a candle;
the other, a crazed palmist,

a preacher with an exploding
Bible. They tell fire

stories and live like saints
off them. They swear

no one was hurt.
At the pitch of the Point

South and Comfort
highballing into Lilesville,

ravens leave the beams
of scorched maples

like a black silk shroud.
Memory configures.

Epiphany

For Sarah Elenor Covington
Born: January 25, 1866
Died: February 8, 1905

It is snowing—
a year and six score, Sarah,
since the few of Anson's twelve hundred
limped back along what was left
of the plank roads used for Yankee tinder.

This Epiphany,
before your tombstone,
I genuflect and listen to flatbeds
squeeze your cathedral of trees
in their stanchions.
Tortured stumps and broken saplings
twist like ramparts
across the whitening slope.

They have sliced your hill away,
revealing your family's 24
X 17 wrought iron cloister
shipped clear from the Stewart Iron Works,
3rd and Culvert Streets,
Cincinnati, Ohio.
The gate is still functional,
its brass ball handle turned green.
A catbird nest clots in its rusted stiles
across which your name, *Covington*, furls.

This place was made for you—
here in the winter of 1905
under slate and buckberry.
Your husband laid his cheek on the rock
at your feet. Your son
was not yet six. Like his father,
who outlived him, he now flanks you.

His stone is fat and modern, yours
and your husband's aged with stonewort.

The loggers have been thorough as Sherman.
Even a hickory which grew through steel
and entered the plot has been taken.
Its belly is pierced like Sebastian's
with Flemish spikes. From Route 109
it appears a fourth marker.
Its stricken heart smells of frankincense.

The Ghosts of Deer

I run in the rain
on the mud flank of 1634

until it dies in the swamp.
There is a bridge and burnt-out

church with nothing
but its doors and block belfry.

Savannah Creek shoulders the road
swerving Anson into Richmond

over Clark and Ingram mountains.
I have prayed for a sign;

and come on foot, barely
clothed at dawn, silently,

never looking away.
For what they are seems burning

among stumps and goblin oaks
stranded in moonscape water

like that instant in the headlights before metal.
The fog is filled with them

unearthing themselves.
Actaeon was turned into a buck

and eaten by his own dogs.
I think of the doe on the Lilesville railhead,

frozen in the giant beam—
little ones dreaming of suicide.

The Woods Behind the Tenant Shack

> ... *it is important to realize where you
> are put on the face of the earth.*
>   —Thomas Merton, *The Sign of Jonas*

The tenant shack faces east.
From its splintered porch
I can see Mount Zion's white steeple
rising from the frozen plowsoles.

No one remembers who lived here—
only whose crop was tended.
Hail pings off the corrugated roof
and rakes the glade above gullies

where beds have swollen, then dried,
swallowing fences now no more
than brittle strings to walk across.
We head south for the confluence

of boulders, theories of map
and compass delicately
balanced between us.
Jersey puts brown eye to the wind

and, with his ounce of Husky blood,
paws the first fork of Cedar Creek,
silvered in blades of ice.
Its banks are shaved,

pocked with moonstone and muscovite.
Morels push out around ferns
and crusted moss on the white root weir.
I plunge into a wall of black stumps

and broken bricks, begin the climb,
disquieted by whispers
and freezing apparitions,
tricked again and again

by the Cedar's serpentine branches.
It is the ruse of fear to hook a man,
build a wall between him and God,
name him lost

when he is somewhere in Anson County—
night falling—with a black dog
on the trail of a hermit thrush.
I hear a whistle

from the old Willoughby Trestle
as a freighter, packed with dead wood,
reckons its milestone and hurtles
through a world of forgetfulness.

The Fox

Eyes closed,
not a mark upon her,
she lay on the gravel shoulder,
sashed to the white line.
The sharp red mask points
toward Savannah Church
and its neon cross.
She does not wake to flatter
the circling crows or follow
the deer line to her rock shelf
where strangled corn haunts
the river among fool's gold
and Pee Dee arrowheads.
In the fables of cunning
there're no accounts of her repose
nor quandary of solitude—
merely morals convincing men
of foxes. The brush lifts
from the tar in the hot
wind like a head of wildfire.

Sneedsborough

> *In the sweat of thy face shalt thou eat bread, till thou return unto the ground; for out of it wast thou taken: for dust thou art, and unto dust shalt thou return*
> —Genesis 3:19

There is no traffic on 1829
north of Whortleberry Creek;
no tracks on the path leading
into Sneedsborough, made legend
by fever and bad seed.
A phantom sun sluices through pine
and jacklegged balsams
spare as Confederate infantry
the year Kilpatrick torched
the ghost town timbers and left
the flames to the Pee Dee flood tide.
The cemetery is all that remains of the town,
seven tombs and a black stone wall
the only architecture:
the Johnsons, the Pearsons;
and, in a row, under cracked granite
slabs and ponderous epitaphs—
each dead at 33—
the Harris brothers and John Hixson,
a Canadian. In this clearing,
prior to these bones and periwinkle,
letters were posted and men loved women;
wayfarers laid down at the Knox Inn
and dreamt of the future.
Genesis was read Ash Wednesdays
with wild promise, sackcloth donned,
gray hair plucked.
Nearly two hundred years ago.
This is all we can know
of their disappearance.

Drought

The corn chants
to be buried in early August.

It prays the land lie fallow
under merciful heaven.

Even the direst love
in the burnt cropheart

and the blood of a boy
farmer could not save it.

There is a farmhouse surrounded
by more hell-colored corn

than one can see beyond.
The cows go unfed

the day of trucks
at Walltown graveyard.

The Deer Stand

Railroad spikes rung
the Sycamore to the deer stand,
thirty feet in the sky—
in the manner of a prudent man:
two-by-sixes and ten-penny common nails;
hard-weathered gray like a barn-side;
a notch for whetted eye and blue barrel,
another for the good book
wherein all things are hidden.
This is where the hunter kneels,
camouflaged, introverted;
alone in a way he cannot be elsewhere,
never mistaking anything
for what it is not.

Relic

In a rick of ice,
the foreleg remains,
sundered at the last joint:
ashe-blonde,
brittle as a wand;
the hoof, an onyx spat
spit-polished in its diamond glaze.
The dogs won't go near it.
They sniff the glassy vetch
where blue droppings bead
and cloven tracks slash
the locked creek bed.
The storm has left a distance
between hunter and kill.
Blood-red shells fill with snow.
Nothing is itself,
but the silence hatching
in the trees.

The Bull

Quail go up at the first crash.
A tulip poplar trembles to the water.
It is the bull, ribald as ever.
Not that he wants to be this way,
but rage is his plaything.
The cows know his curse.
They'd rather forget him.
Today he's demolishing the river bank:
old, a trifle sway-backed,
self-conscious as a graying power-lifter;
up to his hams in mud and buck-tallow,
fuming like an idling Bushhog.
His bastinado head has a near-charming
heaviness, a lovelorn slowness
in the eyes that seems to smile cleverly
as if drumming up his history.
Red clay drapes him.
His sleep is riven by toreadors.
His speed is so unusual—
an army driving thunder,
a black slash across the corn.

Burn Season

> *God talks in the tress.*
> —Thomas Merton, *The Sign of Jonas*

All day chainsaws
ring us and rave their litany
of cut and cut.
There can be no tomorrow.
It is five o'clock and already
the icy moon tethers above
the church of Mount Zion.
We see it from our bedroom.
Its white, spike steeple
points toward heaven.
Its clapboard walls are like snow,
much with us—a winter Purgatory.
Smoke fills the house with musk.
Ants spill from the wood
at the first trickle of flame.
Beneath the buckling bark,
grubs and glowworms disintegrate.
Forget that dirt is the last refuge.
In the split pit of wood so sharp
it sparked at the maul,
I have found chain,
barbed wire,
a hatchet head,
even a swatch of calico,
a coffin nail and small bone.
We live in the trees, without knowing;
we live in the fire.

Possums

They own those eyes
on the midnight shoulder.
They're the stumps
that move from the tussocks,
the sickening black bump
in the chassis.
There's no predicting what they'll do.
They sacrifice themselves
to the fender
with embarrassed looks, snouts
tucked apologetically
into blue-grey fur.
Their afterthought lives
are easily begrudged;
well-meant in all likelihood,
yet ill-equipped to cross the highway.
Mornings they take turns at death,
in wet fetal bundles, curled
on county blacktop.

Entering an Abandoned House

There is no electricity
in the porcelain spools
above jackknifed gutters
where three buzzards leer
like black question marks:
their version of see, speak and hear no evil,
their *Once upon a time* ...

The door is thrown wide
on broken hinges. Batting
and Penzoil cans clot in the mud yard
among renegade clumps of daffodils
and snowdrops, trumpet vines,
viburnum gone haywire.
Corn mummifies in the bottom stubble.
The privy gapes.

The owl is at vespers.
His ironic *who* is second-sensed.
A spendthrift moon levitates.
The whippoorwill insists beyond count
that he is the whippoorwill.

Inside,
light on the dying wallpaper
eyes every tiptoe.
A half-eaten *Pilgrim's Progress*,
forty years overdrawn from the Anson Library,
sures a lame table.
A chair sits at its unfinished toil.
On the floor is an inch of chaff
and a heart-shaped mortuary fan, inscribed:
The spirit is willing,
but the flesh is weak.

Not a thing is prodigal here.
Abandonment has completed this house,
made mystery its intentions.
Like God,
it is inscrutable.

Sundown at the Ballast Pits

The sun saws the ridge in half,
sucking hills of peach trees
into its jagged side.
Bony, arthritic,
trunks bandaged,
they line up holding pale blossoms
in their tangles like an army
surrendering. Tonight
a killing frost threatens.
Two hours at twenty-nine degrees
and they're finished.
Steam shovels keep claw faces
to the quarry heart,
gorging on granite and quartzite.
Dozers and monster lorries
move the earth out of itself.
The sky purples
from Walltown to Gum Springs.
Telephone poles stretch
like crosses in the rock water.
This could be the end—
this terrain,
this obvious brink.

The Sabbath

for Joan

I find her swaying
in the window, shrouded
in lace curtains, singing
nocturnes, arms raised

like a headstrong Pentecostal's.
Today is the Sabbath
and we are filled with the word.
Our house summons gladness,

marshaling for a new spirit.
The firmament is plum purple.
Within it hides heaven
and a hailstorm that will tear down

houses, but pass over us.
Half mile away,
across the green dazzle of May wheat,
an enclave stands at departure

before Mount Zion Church.
Wondering what others pray for,
we take a slow turn over the planks.
Two months into the quickening,

we live in a limbo of lunar charts,
sooth and wives' tales
wherein the pregnant woman
is legend, lore, the storyteller's

muse and gospel, a mandala
subjected to all manner of light
and conjecture to learn
the secret of spit and image.

The gathering storm holds us
in its omniscient eye.
Lightning fires
like a flashbulb freezing

congregants and dancers
in the same frame of benediction.
Just beyond our darkening glass,
horses kneel in the wheat field.

The George Washington Little House

Even in its day
the house was modest—
kept neither for romance nor progeny,
but stealth and utility.

Two storeys of tongue and groove
pine pinned on granite.
Boozy shotgun hall.
Twin flues. Tin roof.

Wood stoves.
Generous, obscure, surrounded
by twelve kinds of thorns
and lapsed Catholic gardens.

I sit with my back to Mount Zion Church
in the room I've learned he sat,
with jug and cronies, bluffing
with a fistful of nothing

before spreading his cards with a laugh
on the table, conjuring
what the heart holds long after
eye or hand: a field

of cotton, white lightning,
an unborn child, the notion
of a wife. Imagine
an unloved man on fire

making his way across the fields
to the Pee Dee, star thistle
and milkweed catching in his wake,
panicked cattle, cedars

going up like monstrous tongues,
copperheads on flame-lit rocks.
I have studied the crypt at Eastview.
It holds the harrowing answer

to the riddle of man and woman
till death do them part.
I account this by candle—
my unwitting séance—

and listen for George's peg-leg clump.
At my feet: charred grooves
his spent cigars have left
in the skewed and gapping poker floor.

Tonight this house tips with frills,
the livery of children.
We've removed the hasps
from the upstairs bedrooms

and reclaimed the seed beds.
Swifts settle the chimney for another summer.
There is no horseshoe
above our unlocked door.

Disaster Pay

Sun rams the black road
through green-gone
and crumbling corn
like a stake through the burning
heart of August.
Engines hackle brown waves
of dead ears and rotting silk,
shocking what can be for fodder.
Now, a season late,
in aborted trickles, rain
comes every fortnight.
Farmers measure razed fields
in disaster pay.

Marriage

Yet hidden in the country such a house
exists unhindered by itself.

No one cares to notice
what appears impoverished.

Man, red; woman, black.
Afraid of nothing but drought,

they ornament the seasons with bells
and pumpkins and ceramic chickens.

They link their wash
on the long line over the furrows

for better, for worse.
Not their land upon which they live and toil—

that swarms the patched house
in growing season and peels back

flat as famine when fallow,
leaving mosquitoes to breed

in the forked prints of deer
and crows as the hawk's bondsmen

above the distant timberline.
Beneath a light on the porch pole

they sit, worn; the radio playing
Heart of My Heart as the terrific silence

limns them against the world:
statues in an endless gallery.

Made things that stare at the moon
beyond sleep's window, not dreaming

of what is wrong, but what is
bedded in bone and hereafter;

and, like beasts hunkering beneath
what now calls their blankets,

pray and kiss and listen
to what they alone can hear

in the strange love borne
on the earthback turning.

Copperhead

The dogs have seen a ghost.
They dance around the demon,
barking with dread at the sexless coils,
the switchblade tongue.
The book insists it's death's look alike.
I'm tempted to let it go about its business,
but it does not fathom mercy.
Snug on its hump of clay and bloodberries,
it begins unraveling.
The puckered skull levitates.
No moon nor fury for this work,
I've merely an inkling of kill or be killed—
a sorry yet orthodox theology.
Like an exorcist, I lift the spade
and pray to the God of murder,
then strike.
All night I dream
of the death-wiggle,
the ghastly heap flip-flopping,
the severed head
inching toward my boot.

A Topography of Snakes

Of poetic name and murderous intent,
they catacomb our fields,
lashing themselves to corn and chokecherry,
draping the shaddock trees,
plumbing our slow green rivers.
We are warm-blooded prey,
yet have chosen a topography of snakes,
beseeching our blood to stiffen
at the night's sudden sibilance.
Of course there is prayer,
but we cannot be shriven
of the snakes of our lives
nor the nightmare of wandering
into flash and fang.
I wake to hack and slash
at the white mouth and sandix patch,
swirling diamonds and amber hourglasses,
the pit between eye and nostril.
They wend toward us like long wet knives.
The stench of vent fluids chokes the air.
We loot nests, smashing eggs,
burning live young,
cauterize lairs with venom-
slaking quick-lime.
Even the innocent
vine and garter snakes are slaughtered.

Easter

They stand like shades
against the skyline:
in resurrection suits
and second-day dresses;
waiting to be gathered and burned
by the first fires of dawn
they have come to believe
will perfect their two-days-planted fruit.
Now like the rush of souls
it leaps across the sky
shredding fog with cerise flames
sudden as tongues.
And there can be no denial
of this white light
that carves fields rife
with wheat and corn,
sculpts holy men behind plows,
draws the harrow and martingale—
nor the flash and raiment of seeds
above the red river mouth.
Behold.

On the Road to White Store

> *What is so real as the cry of a child?*
> *A rabbit's cry may be wilder*
> *But it has no soul.*
> —Sylvia Plath

It is you on the road
to White Store, a town
now no more than boarded
white store and green sign
on a stick; a reliquary
of charred brick columns
where deer dance on the blades
of secret lives, buckshot
nightmares; and the poor
couple in tatters.

There is a little boy
at the window of block shed.
His hands are black against the pane.
His shirts dry in a burdock tree.
A hawk rises from the yellow shoulder,
a rabbit in its talons.
Stray dogs deny
love is a sure thing.
God holds you
in His stereopticon.

Cows

They are there in the night
when without light there is no color
to green the black fodder.

Unknown, identically nameless,
though christened by the imperceptible
dwindling of those before them,

pastured with a claw-foot tub
from which to drink and their bodies'
incessant machinery.

Twice a year the bull appears; and twice
a year there is the barbed cuss
which tears the calving mothers.

The omnivore drinks the milk,
eats the flesh, never ponders
what is Christ-like

in the black-washed cow:
white face glued to the angus stump,
shoulder high in a still mud pond,

agape at the salt block and milo rick.
Their thirst is exquisite.
They sidle away like convicts.

The Ingram Plantation

for the Davises

A logging chain wraps the roadmost oak.
Beneath it on two rock scrolls

sits a hundred pounds of granite,
inscribed: *Ingram Plantation,*

Since 1769.
A Sabbath hush enshrines the house,

haunted as are all houses
left to their histories, filmed

and peripheral in the spectral light
of souls returning to the little

which can be known of things.
The rooms choose silence,

opening on rheumatoid jambs
like the fragile spine

of the family Bible.
Black doorknobs eye the turnkey.

Ivy pours through amnesiac windows.
The Ingrams dream

in their ancestral grove,
slave stones scattered like seeds

at their feet. Across the river,
fields are burning.

The Contemplatives of Grassy Island

for Steve and Fred

Through winter wheat and cherry,
we trek with proper boots and bottle,
the plat between us; while above
a Shrovetide horoscope absconds

with the future. It is said
the world will end in our time,
that modernity and contrition
have clashed like angry prophets,

and we are no longer pitied by our betters.
We squat in the rock flume,
waiting for deer,
chanting like Gregorians.

Flint and mica catch the full moon
roaring in our eyes.
Sycamores lean over the creek bed
like long silver women.

A distant ocean measures the wind.
Bamboo quivers with night birds.
Children sleep.
The sky is groomed for funeral:

black dress, string of pearls,
Lenten hush as the Dog Star rises
over Grassy Island, teasing the ghosts
of Yeats and Emerson and all the nibbled

souls in Purgatory. Yet
on we go naming things, drinking
to dominion through faults
most grievous, though devout;

mount a buck skull to confound Lucifer
at the south fork of the Cedar;
then march across the red gleaned fields,
enter the silo to sing and dance,

play charades and blackjack,
recite the Confiteor and study heaven
through Steve Carey's telescope.
Up through the opening,

the sky fills with beat angels—
cool old guys with beards and cigarettes
who wink at us and hit joyful
licks on battered harps.

Leaving Anson County

> *Now. Is this life or not?*
> —Alice Walker, *The Color Purple*

The hardest thing we do
is leave our middle ground,

this unlikely blade of life we've honed.
We read short things,

thaw the frozen larder;
walk in small circles,

window to window, reminded
memory is the rival of presence,

the riddle of locus
in the thicket of time.

The least moon beats into the east
which hides our destiny

in epistolary ruin.
Mount Zion Church gleams,

locked and beckoning.
Never have I entered it,

yet it's the frontispiece of my heart.
Every day I put mouth to stone

in the sunset paint of Ingram Mountain,
pray for that Biblical surety

graced by fire
and chance blindness.

We spin for the last time
over roads splayed with tektite

and thistle abloom
like wine in horned cups.

This is the purple—
the exultation of the ordinary,

our lives in an instant
of light and elevation

whiter than angels.
The parting is thorough as film.

Timber grinds up and down
the Andrew Jackson Highway.

JOSEPH BATHANTI is the Poet Laureate of North Carolina. He is the author of seven books of poetry: *Communion Partners, Anson County, The Feast of All Saints, This Metal (nominated for the National Book Award), Land of Amnesia,* and *Restoring Sacred Art* (winner of the Roanoke Chowan Prize), and *Sonnets of the Cross*. A new collection of poems, *Concertina*, is forthcoming from Mercer University Press. His novel, *East Liberty*, won the 2001 Carolina Novel Award. His latest novel, *Coventry*, won the 2006 Novello Literary Award. His book of stories, *The High Heart*, won the 2006 Spokane Prize. His collection of personal essays, *Half of What I Say Is Meaningless*, winner of the 2012 Will D. Campbell Award for Creative Nonfiction, is forthcoming from Mercer University Press. He is the recipient of Literature Fellowships from the North Carolina Arts Council in 1994 (poetry) and 2009 (fiction); the Samuel Talmadge Ragan Award, presented annually for outstanding contributions to the Fine Arts of North Carolina over an extended period; the Linda Flowers Prize; the Sherwood Anderson Award; the Barbara Mandigo Kelly Peace Poetry Prize; the 2011 Donald Murray Prize; the 2012 Ragan-Rubin Award; the 2013 Mary Frances Hobson Prize; and others. Bathanti is Professor of Creative Writing at Appalachian State University.

Cover Artist **AGNIESZKA PIECHOCINSKA** is a primary school teacher and amateur photographer from Osiek, a village in southern Poland. She finds inspiration in nature and small, seemingly insignificant objects, especially old ones. She also loves abandoned, ruined buildings with all their stories and secrets.

For five years she has been sharing her photos on DeviantArt at piechot.deviantart.com.

www.ingramcontent.com/pod-product-compliance
Lightning Source LLC
Chambersburg PA
CBHW022109040426
42451CB00007B/190